A RESOUNDING TINKLE

A Play in One Act

by
N. F. Simpson

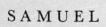

SAMUEL  FRENCH

LONDON

NEW YORK   TORONTO   SYDNEY   HOLLYWOOD

I S B N 0 573 02229 1

A RESOUNDING TINKLE

Produced at the Royal Court Theatre, London, on the
2nd April, 1958, with the following cast of characters:

(in the order of their appearance)

BRO PARADOCK	*Nigel Davenport*
MIDDIE PARADOCK	*Wendy Craig*
UNCLE TED	*Sheila Ballantine*

Directed by WILLIAM GASKILL
Décor by TAZEENA FIRTH

*The action of the Play passes during an evening in the
living-room of the Paradocks' suburban home*

Time—the present

A RESOUNDING TINKLE

SCENE—*The living-room of the Paradocks' suburban home. Evening.*

A door back C *leads to a small entrance hall, where coats and hats are hanging. There is a window* R *of the door, from which anyone standing on the front doorstep can be seen obliquely. A window* R *looks out on to the garden. The fireplace is* L. *A sofa stands* LC *with a small table* L *of it, on which there is a radio-receiver. A low, coffee-table stands in front of the sofa. On it, there are some rug-making materials. There is an armchair* RC *and a sideboard up* R. *Several bottles are on the sideboard. Small tables stand down* R *and down* L. *There is a telephone on the table down* L. *Built-in bookshelves fill the wall* L *of the door. A standard lamp is above the window* R. *In the hall there is a hall-cupboard and a hatstand with hats and coats on it. Other suitable dressing may be added at the discretion of the Producer.*

(See the Ground Plan at the end of the Play)

When the CURTAIN *rises, it is not yet dark, and the window curtains are undrawn. A fire is burning in the grate.* BRO *and* MIDDIE PARADOCK *have just come in. A shopping basket full of books is on the coffee table. Both* BRO *and* MIDDIE *are staring out of the window* R *into the garden.*

MIDDIE. It'll have to stay out.

BRO (*turning away from the window*) What are the measurements?

MIDDIE (*continuing to stare through the window*) You don't need measurements. A thing that size in a semi!

BRO (*moving to the sideboard*) I thought we were living in a bungalow. (*He picks up two small adjustable spanners from the sideboard*)

MIDDIE. People think you're trying to go one better than everybody else.

BRO. What are these doing here? When did we order adjustable spanners?

MIDDIE (*without turning*) They were samples.

BRO. What do they think we want with two?

MIDDIE. (*turning away from the window and beginning to put books from the shopping basket on to the bookshelf*) One of them is probably for loosening things.

BRO. You can do that with any spanner.

MIDDIE (*with a handful of small identical books*) I've brought in some more of these in case Uncle Ted comes. I expect he'll ask for critical essays with his coffee.

BRO (*after a pause*) There's no difference between them. You can use either of them for tightening and you can use either of them for loosening.

(MIDDIE *puts the last book on the shelf, picks up the basket and moves to the door*)

MIDDIE. One is probably bigger than the other or something.

(MIDDIE *exits up* C *to* L, *leaving the door open*)

BRO. They're *adjustable*, Middie. (*He puts the spanners on the sideboard, goes to the armchair* RC, *picks up a newspaper, sits and reads*)

MIDDIE (*off*) Or smaller or something.

BRO. The plain fact is that we don't need adjustable spanners and are never likely to. (*He pauses*) It would be interesting to know what would have happened if *I'd* answered the door and let them foist adjustable spanners on to us.

MIDDIE (*off*) We don't have to use them if we don't like them.

BRO (*after a pause*) We shall have them unloading a complete tool-kit on us before we know where we are.

MIDDIE (*off*) They won't be round again.

BRO. I hope you're right—that's all I can say.

MIDDIE (*off*) I wish it were.

(MIDDIE *enters up* C *from* L, *and as though attracted compulsively towards it, crosses to the window* R)

I wish that were all you could say. Except that then we'd have you saying it all day long, I suppose, like a mentally deficient parakeet. (*She looks steadily through the window*)

BRO. What a typical woman's remark. A parakeet saying the same thing over and over again wouldn't necessarily be mentally deficient. If that's all it's been taught how can it say anything different?

MIDDIE. Look at it.

BRO. It may be educationally subnormal—but that's another matter.

MIDDIE. Look at its great ears flapping about.

BRO (*after a pause*) It's only once a year for goodness sake.

MIDDIE. Surely they know by now what size we always have.

BRO. Perhaps they've sent us the wrong one.

MIDDIE (*crossing above the armchair to the sofa*) It's big enough for a hotel. (*She picks up a magazine from the coffee-table and sits on the sofa*) If you had a hotel or a private school or something you wouldn't need a thing that size. (*She looks through the magazine*)

BRO. I suppose not.

MIDDIE. And supposing it goes berserk in the night? I'm not getting up to it.

BRO. Why should it go berserk any more than a smaller one?

MIDDIE. We shall have old Mrs Stencil round again if it does—threatening us with the R.S.P.C.A.

BRO. You should have been in when they came with it, then you could have queried the measurements.

MIDDIE. I can't think what we're going to call it. We can't call it Mr Trench again.

BRO. The only time we've not called it Mr Trench was three years ago when we had to make do with a giraffe.

MIDDIE. And look at the fuss we had before they'd take it in part exchange.

BRO. Of course they made a fuss. There was something wrong with it.

(MIDDIE *puts the magazine on the coffee-table, then picks up her rug-making materials and works on the rug. She does this intermittently throughout the evening*)

MIDDIE. Imagine calling a clumsy great thing that size Mr Trench.

BRO. Why not?

MIDDIE. We can't go on year after year calling it Mr Trench.

BRO. You talk as if it were the same animal every time.

MIDDIE. You can hear the neighbours, can't you? They'll think we never launch out.

BRO. I know what you want to call it.

MIDDIE. It looks all the time as if we're hard up for a name to give the animal.

BRO. You want to call it Oedipus Rex, don't you?

MIDDIE. It's better than Mr Trench year after year. At least it sounds as if we knew what was going on in the world.

BRO (*contemptuously*) Oedipus Rex! (*He wags a finger archly through the window*) Ah, ah! Only the *edible* blooms, remember, Oedipus.

MIDDIE. If you say it in that tone of voice—of course it sounds ridiculous.

BRO. Oedipus! Not all your weight on that glass, eh?

MIDDIE. Anything would sound ridiculous if you said it like that.

BRO. It isn't Mr Trench we want a change from.

MIDDIE. The only thing to do is ring up the Zoo. Tell them to come and collect it.

BRO. And be without an elephant at all?

MIDDIE. Tell them to come and collect it and the sooner the better. I'd rather not have one.

BRO. That's only your point of view.

MIDDIE. We did without one the year we had a giraffe instead.

BRO. I know we did without one the year we had a giraffe instead. And look at the trouble we had getting it changed. I don't want that all over again.

MIDDIE. It's the R.S.P.C.A. I'm worried about.

BRO. They haven't been round yet. In any case you wouldn't get the Zoo at this time. They'll be closed.

MIDDIE. I don't know why they couldn't send us what we asked for in the first place.

BRO. Is it any use trying to get hold of Eddie on the phone?

MIDDIE. Yes. Ring Eddie up. Or Nora. Nora'd be sure to know what to do. They used to keep pigeons and things. They had a room full of nothing else but different kinds of birds when they were all living at number eighty-nine, and white mice and things.

BRO. It'll have to stay outside tonight.

MIDDIE. I'm not having it in the kitchen, if that's what you're leading up to.

BRO. If it starts straying all over the place during the night we shall have the R.S.P.C.A. making a lot of difficulties.

MIDDIE. Not if we get it changed first thing. Get on to Nora.

BRO. If we're getting it changed first thing in the morning, where's the sense in thinking up a name like Oedipus Rex for it now?

MIDDIE. Because I'm not calling it Mr Trench six years running. You can if you like. I'm not.

BRO. I didn't want to call it Mr Trench the year it was a giraffe. That was your idea. It was your idea it would make a pleasant change to give the name to a giraffe instead of an elephant. Now you complain about calling it Mr Trench six years running.

MIDDIE. I think we'd be better off without it.

BRO. How would we?

MIDDIE. I do really. I think we'd be better off without. We've done nothing except bicker ever since they came with it.

BRO. We weren't in when they came with it.

MIDDIE. That's the whole point.

(*Both relapse into silence.* BRO *reads his paper.* After a few moments he looks up)

BRO. If we're going to change the name at all, I can't see what you've got against "Hodge" for that matter.

MIDDIE. "Hodge" is all right for a monkey.

BRO. We'll go through some names and see what we can agree on. "Hodge."

MIDDIE. "Hodge" for a monkey. "Gush" for an elephant.

BRO. "Admiral Benbow."

MIDDIE. "Hiram B. Larkspur."

BRO. "Playboy."

MIDDIE. "Killed-with-kindness Corcoran."

BRO. "New-wine-into-old-bottles Backhouse."

MIDDIE. " 'Tis-pity-she's-a-whore Hignett."

BRO. "Lucifer."

MIDDIE. "Stonehenge."

BRO. "Haunch."

(*There is a pause*)

MIDDIE⎫
BRO ⎬ (*almost simultaneously*) "Splinter."

BRO. Thank goodness we can agree on something. Now I can ring Eddie. (*He puts his paper on the floor, rises, crosses to the telephone down* L, *lifts the receiver and dials a number*)

MIDDIE. Why ring Eddie when you've got Nora who's had some experience with animals? She could probably suggest something.

BRO. So you keep saying.

MIDDIE. Well?

BRO (*into the telephone*) Is that Mrs Mortice?... Oh... Yes, will you? Tell her Bro Paradock would like a word with her. (*He waits*)

MIDDIE. You've decided to ring Nora, then?

BRO (*ignoring Middie; into the telephone*) Hallo . . . Nora?... Yes, thank you, Norah. And how are you?... Oh?... And what's that, Nora?... A what?... No! I can't believe it. Hold on a moment, Nora. Wait till I fetch Middie to the phone.

MIDDIE. Don't tell me they've got ours.

BRO (*to Middie*) It's her snake. It's too short.

MIDDIE. Too short for what? (*She rises, moves to Bro and takes the receiver from him*)

BRO. She says they're worried about the R.S.P.C.A. (*He moves* LC)

MIDDIE (*into the telephone*) Nora? . . . Yes, Bro was telling me. Isn't it maddening? . . . Yes . . . Yes . . . Yes, and do you know they've done exactly the same with us . . . No—about ten times too big. You'd think they'd know by now, wouldn't you? A thing that size in a semi of all things.

BRO. This is a bungalow, for the fiftieth time.

MIDDIE (*to Bro*) Oh, for God's sake! (*Into the telephone*) No, Nora, I was talking to Bro. He won't have it we're living in a semi. If I've got the deeds out once to show him, I've got them out a hundred times . . .

BRO. I wouldn't have bought the place without looking pretty closely . . .

MIDDIE (*into the telephone*) Just a moment, Nora. He's got to have his say out.

BRO. I wouldn't have bought it without looking pretty closely at the deeds to see if there was any mention of its being semi-detached. It's one of the things I always look for.

MIDDIE (*into the telephone*) I'm sorry, Nora. I've started Bro off on his hobby-horse again . . .

BRO. You just read things into them once you've made up your mind.

MIDDIE (*into the telephone*) He's got a thing about this being a bungalow, Nora. He hasn't set foot upstairs since we moved in . . . Exactly, Nora . . . It's just the same with us, of course. We're stuck with the thing like you . . . We shan't get the Zoo at this time . . . We shall just have to keep it till the morning . . . Not indoors, no. We've got it out at the back . . . Yes, I should think so, Nora . . . You're perfectly justified . . .

(BRO *tries to attract Middie's attention*)

BRO. Why not ask her if she'd like to have Mr Trench and we'll take the snake off her?

MIDDIE (*to Bro*) What? (*Into the telephone*) No, it's

something Bro just said, Nora. I think he's thought of something. I'll get him to tell you. (*She puts her hand over the mouthpiece. To Bro*) You talk to her; she's on about this snake of hers.

(BRO *takes the receiver from* MIDDIE, *who moves* LC)

BRO (*into the telephone*) What do you say to that, Nora? . . . How about it? . . . Oh, I thought Middie told you. It was just an idea I had—I thought perhaps we could help each other out if I came round with our Mr Trench and took the snake off you . . . Are you? . . . Yes—Middie wants to change the name of ours this year . . . "Oedipus Rex" . . . Of course it is, Nora—and for an elephant this size. Middie doesn't seem to see that . . . Yes . . . No—don't bother about changing the name, Nora. We can do all that ourselves when we get it home . . . "Bees' Wedding"? . . . Oh, yes. I should think that must look rather good on a snake. Wait a moment, Nora—I'll ask Middie. (*To Middie*) She's called her snake "Bees' Wedding". What do you think? Shall I tell her to take it off the snake and keep it for Mr Trench when I take him round?

MIDDIE. That'll mean we shall have to find a name to fit the snake out with.

BRO. Let's see what "Bees' Wedding" looks like on Mr Trench, first. (*Into the telephone*) Hold on a moment, Nora.

(MIDDIE *and* BRO *look out for a few moments through the window* R *into the garden*)

What do you think?

MIDDIE. Wait till he turns round.

BRO. Remember she's got the upstairs as well.

MIDDIE. Yes—well, it's better, anyway, than "Mr Trench" for him.

BRO. I'll just tell her to keep "Bees' Wedding" for Mr Trench, then.

MIDDIE. Ask her about "Mr Trench" on the snake; see what she thinks.

BRO (*into the telephone*) Nora? . . . Yes, it fits beautifully . . . Tailor-made, Nora . . . Would you, Nora? I

was going to ask you if you wouldn't mind doing that . . .
(*To Middie*) She's trying it on the snake, now.

> (*There is a knock at the front door.*
>
> MIDDIE *exits up* C, *closing the door behind her.* BRO *waits, humming to himself*)

(*Into the telephone*) Oh, splendid, Nora . . . No—no
trouble at all . . . That's better still . . . In about half
an hour, then . . . Yes. Good-bye, Nora. (*He replaces
the receiver*)

> (MIDDIE *enters up* C)

MIDDIE (*moving to the sofa*) It was lucky we rang her
up. (*She sits and works on her rug*)

BRO. Did she say how short this snake was?

MIDDIE. She didn't give any measurements, if that's
what you mean.

BRO. I thought perhaps you might have thought to
ask her what the measurements were.

MIDDIE. Why didn't you ask her for the measurements
yourself, as far as that goes?

BRO. How was I to know whether you'd asked
already?

MIDDIE. You heard me talking to her.

> (*There is a pause*)

BRO. Who was that at the door?

MIDDIE. It was two comedians. They wanted to come
in and amuse us.

BRO. That's the second time this week. Where are
they now?

MIDDIE. I sent them next door.

BRO. Not to Mrs Gride?

MIDDIE. I said we've already been amused, thank you.

BRO. Mrs Gride is going to be pleased—having
comedians foisted on to her.

MIDDIE. She wasn't above sending the undertaker in
to us, was she?

> (*There is a pause*)

Bro. Were both of them funny?

Middie. How should I know?

Bro. I just wondered if one was funnier than the other.

Middie. They just asked if they could come in and be comic for a few minutes.

(*There is a pause*)

The last time we had them in here I was picking up jokes in the Hoover for days afterwards.

Bro. I suppose they didn't say how comic they were going to be?

Middie. I didn't ask them.

(*There is a pause*)

Bro. I'm wondering if we've done the right thing about this snake of Nora's.

Middie. You haven't done it yet.

Bro. What happens if it turns out to be about two inches long?

Middie. You can always have them lengthened.

Bro. I know you can have them lengthened. But you don't get the thickness then. (*He crosses to the door and opens it*) What have you done with my gumboots?

Middie. What do you want gumboots for to go down the road a few doors with an elephant? Where are your other shoes?

Bro (*standing in the doorway*) These are my other shoes I've got on.

Middie. And I should come straight back with Mr Trench. We don't want Mrs Stencil asking a lot of questions.

Bro. I notice you've agreed to keep "Mr Trench" for it now you know it's a snake.

Middie. And what are you going to bring it back in? You can't trail a snake on a lead like a canary.

Bro. In any case I thought we'd settled on "Hodge" for a name.

Middie. "Hodge" for a jackal. "Gush" for an anaconda.

Bro. "Admiral Benbow."

Middie. "Hiram B. Larkspur."

Bro. "Playboy."

Middie. You're just thinking up names at random.

Bro. How else can I think them up?

Middie. You can wait till you've seen how short it is.

(*There is a pause.* Bro *turns to go out of the door*)

Bro. I hate this job.

Middie. You say that every year.

Bro. I've never had to do it before.

Middie. You say it about other things.

(Bro *exits to the hall and re-enters almost at once*)

Bro. If it comes to that, how do you know it *is* an anaconda?

Middie. What else would it be? We shall have the R.S.P.C.A. round while you stand there.

Bro. Good God!

(Bro *exits to the hall and shuts the door behind him*)

Middie (*moving her head slowly from side to side*) "Admiral Benbow!"

(Bro, *after a few moments, re-enters. His coat collar is turned up. He turns it down and shakes water from his jacket, then picks up his newspaper, sits in the armchair and reads*)

You're not back already?

Bro. I'm not going in this rain.

Middie. It's barely started yet.

Bro. I'm not going out in it. I haven't got a hat suitable for going out in the rain. You know that.

Middie. You've got an eyeshield.

Bro. You gave it away.

Middie. I don't mean the one I gave away. I mean the one you wear for tennis.

Bro. But that's to keep the sun out of my eyes.

Middie. Couldn't you wear it back to front?

(*A knock is heard at the front door*)

(*She rises and moves to the door*) That would be too ingenious for you, I suppose.

(MIDDIE *exits to the hall.* BRO *reads the newspaper.*

MIDDIE *returns with an unopened telegram, which she hands to Bro*)

(*She sits on the sofa and works at the rug*) It's Uncle Ted and that motor-scooter again I expect. I shall be glad when we see the last of that craze.

BRO (*opening the telegram*) What's he up to this time?

MIDDIE. He's probably been parking his motor-scooter on that piece of waste ground again behind Rachmaninov's Second Piano Concerto.

BRO. Who does that belong to?

MIDDIE. It doesn't belong to anybody. It's just a piece of waste ground.

BRO. Then they can't stop him parking his motor-scooter on it if it doesn't belong to anyone.

MIDDIE. I suppose they can't.

BRO (*reading the telegram*) "Arriving Euston twelve-ten send sandwiches." (*He ponders*) The last time we had a telegram like this it was worded very differently.

MIDDIE. Perhaps we ought to take it back and get it seen to.

BRO. No. If they start playing about with the wording we shan't know where we are. It's in code. We should never decipher it.

MIDDIE. How can you tell whether it's in code?

BRO. There isn't any way of telling. Either it is or it isn't. This one is.

MIDDIE. Thank heaven for that, then. We can set our minds at rest.

BRO (*rising*) Lucky I spotted it. (*He puts the telegram on the coffee-table*)

MIDDIE (*glancing through the window*) Do you know it's stopped raining?

BRO. I'll get across to Nora's then with the elephant. (*He moves to the door*) What have you done with my gumboots?

MIDDIE. What do you want gumboots for to go down

the road a few doors with an elephant? Where are your other shoes?

BRO. These are my other shoes I've got on.

MIDDIE. And I should come straight back with Mr Trench. We don't want Mrs Stencil asking a lot of questions.

BRO. I notice you've agreed to call it "Mr Trench" now you know it's a snake.

MIDDIE. And what are you going to bring it back in? You can't trail a snake on a lead like a canary.

BRO. In any case I thought we'd settled on "Hodge" for a name.

MIDDIE. "Hodge" for an antelope. "Gush" for a boa constrictor.

BRO. "Admiral Benbow."

MIDDIE. "Hiram B. Larkspur."

BRO. "Playboy."

MIDDIE. We've been through all this before. For goodness' sake pull yourself together. We shall have the R.S.P.C.A. round while you stand there.

BRO. Perhaps we shall. Perhaps we shan't.

(BRO *exits.* MIDDIE *rises, goes to the fireplace, tidies the hearth and puts some coal on the fire.*

BRO *re-enters. He seems to have been thrown momentarily off balance, and speaks as though dazed*)

There was somebody at the door.

MIDDIE. Who?

BRO (*moving to* R *of the sofa*) I told him he'd better wait. (*He pauses*) He wants me to form a government.

MIDDIE. What does he look like?

BRO. He says he's working through the street directory.

(MIDDIE, *who has sized up the situation in her own way, quickly completes the tidying of the hearth, picks up two bottles from under the table* L *of the sofa, and hands them to Bro*)

MIDDIE (*motioning towards the sideboard*) You might do something about all these bottles. What does it look like if the Cabinet arrive suddenly?

B

BRO. He was wearing an old raincoat.

MIDDIE. He was very likely trying it on for size. (*She smooths the loose cover on the sofa*)

BRO (*beginning to move abstractedly among the bottles*) What would he be doing trying an old raincoat on for size?

MIDDIE. It might not be as old as the one he had before. (*She pauses*) The coat he had before may have been in tatters for all you or I know. It may have been black with grease.

BRO. I doubt it. I very much doubt it.

MIDDIE. Or mud or something.

BRO. Mud possibly. But not grease.

MIDDIE. Why not grease? (*She goes into the hall, leaving the door open, and is seen foraging among the coats*)

BRO (*crossing to the fireplace*) There's no grounds for thinking it's grease any more than mud. (*He takes a pipe from the mantelpiece and begins thoughtfully filling it*) How can I start forming a Government at six o'clock in the evening?

(MIDDIE *comes in to* R *of the sofa holding up a torn and dirty raincoat*)

MIDDIE. Look at this thing. How do you know his mightn't have been in a worse state than this one? Look —what's that but grease? Look at the sleeves. And his was probably as bad or worse. (*She returns the coat to the hall*)

BRO. How can I start forming a Government at six o'clock in the evening?

MIDDIE (*coming into the room*) You'd be saying the same thing if it were six o'clock in the morning. (*She closes the door, moves to the sofa and sits*)

BRO. It's the Prime Minister's job.

MIDDIE. That's one way of shelving your responsibilities, I suppose.

BRO. It's not a question of shelving anything. I just don't want the job. And in any case where would I begin forming a Government? We don't know anybody.

MIDDIE. You could make a start by asking Uncle Ted

when he gets here. And in the meantime there's a man at the door waiting for your answer.

(*There is a pause*)

Bro. How do I know he isn't wanted by the police?
Middie. Why should he be?
Bro. If he is we ought to turn him over.

(Middie *rises and peers from behind a curtain through the window next to the door*)

Middie (*coming away*) If he's a criminal, he's in plain clothes. That's all I can say. (*She sits on the sofa*)
Bro. I'm going to turn him over and be on the safe side.
Middie. You may never get another chance to form a Government.
Bro. That goes for anything I ever choose not to do.
Middie. So what's it to be?
Bro (*crossing to the door*) I'll see what he's got to say.

(Bro *exits, closing the door.* Middie *works at her rug.*
Bro *re-enters, goes to the armchair, picks up his newspaper and sits.* Middie *waits expectantly*)

(*Casually*) It was someone having a joke.
Middie. I would have recognized him through the window.
Bro. He was disguising his voice. (*He pauses, glancing through his newspaper*) He said he thought I looked like Gladstone.
Middie. And did you?
Bro. That sort of thing cuts no ice with me.
Middie. You should have led him on. You should have pretended to think it was eighteen sixty-eight.
Bro. I was all of a piece with his asking me to form a Government in the first place.
Middie. I hope you didn't start saying, Your mission was to pacify Ireland?
Bro. It cuts no more ice with me, that sort of thing, than Gladstone would have done if I'd been Queen

Victoria. And God knows there's little enough of the Empress of India about me.

MIDDIE. It would have been playing into his hands to say, Your mission was to pacify Ireland.

BRO. I know it would have been playing into his hands.

MIDDIE. I can't think why I didn't recognize him.

BRO. I've told you he was having a joke with us.

MIDDIE. I suppose he thought he could talk you round. Like last time when they had you voting for some candidate who refused to stand.

BRO. He said he was round canvassing for the Whigs.

MIDDIE. You should have let him come in for a few moments to try your overcoat on.

BRO. He'd never have got into it.

MIDDIE. Exactly.

BRO. He was broader across the shoulders than I am. He probably still is. I doubt whether he could even have worn it like a cloak.

MIDDIE. You don't see what I'm leading up to, do you?

BRO. It would have looked thoroughly ridiculous on him.

MIDDIE. I know your overcoat would have been too small for him. Of course it would have looked ridiculous. It looks ridiculous on you most of the time. But don't you see that if he'd tried it on in here, I could have seen at a glance he wasn't a man of your build? After a time I might have been able to narrow it down still further. As it is I don't know what to think. (*She pauses*) What happened about the Government? Did you agree to form one or not?

BRO. He didn't approach me any more.

MIDDIE. I see. It didn't occur to you to raise it?

BRO. I've no desire whatever to form a Government.

MIDDIE. And while you're sitting there not wanting to form a Government, he's probably next door. Asking Mrs Gride's husband.

BRO. He's very likely forgotten all about it by now.

MIDDIE. If he's forgotten all about it already, how do we know he was genuine in the first place? It could

have been any old Tom, Dick or Harry asking you to
form a Government. (*She pauses*) It looks to me as if
you've let yourself in for something with your bland
assumptions about it being someone having a joke with us.

(UNCLE TED, *a young woman, elegantly dressed, enters
quietly with the obvious intention of surprising* BRO *and*
MIDDIE *who continue talking, unaware of her presence. She
stands waiting for one of them to look up*)

You'll be getting a man round before you know where
you are with papers to prove it's eighteen sixty-eight.

BRO. But not that I'm Gladstone.

MIDDIE. If it's eighteen sixty-eight, it makes precious
little difference whether you're Gladstone or not. (*She
looks up, sees Uncle Ted and is momentarily speechless with
astonishment*) Uncle Ted! (*She rises*) Why, you've changed
your sex! (*She draws Uncle Ted down* C)

(UNCLE TED *strikes an attitude which invites appraisal.*
BRO *rises*)

You look lovely—doesn't he, Bro? But why ever
didn't you let us know?

UNCLE TED. Surely you got the telegram I sent you?
(*She crosses to the fireplace, removes her gloves, looks in the
mirror over the mantelpiece and pats her hair*)

BRO. We got one—but it was in code.

UNCLE TED (*turning*) Oh, no! What a fool of a man!

(BRO *reacts*)

No—not you, Bro. It's that idiot at the post office.

BRO. We were wondering if you were having trouble
with the motor-scooter again.

UNCLE TED. I told him when I handed it in that it
wasn't to go off without being decoded first.

MIDDIE. They're not very reliable.

UNCLE TED (*putting her gloves and handbag on the coffee-
table*) I gave him the code number and everything. It
isn't as if he had to break it down letter by letter himself
or anything. So I suppose you hadn't quite expected
such a change? (*She sits on the sofa*)

MIDDIE. We shall get used to it. It just seems funny calling you "Uncle Ted". But you must be dying for a read.

UNCLE TED. Yes, I'd love a book, Middie. I haven't opened one since I got into the train at four o'clock this morning.

(MIDDIE *goes to the bookshelves, takes out a number of books and arranges them on a tray.* BRO *sits in the armchair*)

BRO. What sort of a journey did you have this time, Uncle Ted?

UNCLE TED. The usual kind, Bro. I just got into the train, and from then onwards it was just a matter of moving in roughly the same direction practically the whole time until I got out of it at Euston.

(MIDDIE *brings the tray of books to Uncle Ted and puts it on the coffee-table*)

Ah, thank you, Middie.

MIDDIE. There are some nice critical essays, if you'd like one of those. Or biography. Or I've got some text-books in the cupboard . . . ?

(UNCLE TED *rises and takes a small book*)

UNCLE TED. No—I think I'll have this book of poems, Middie. I feel as if I could really do justice to a good poem after travelling up to Euston since four o'clock this morning. Thank you, Middie. (*She sits on the left arm of the sofa and reads silently and intently*)

MIDDIE (*crossing to Bro; in an undertone*) I wonder what the next craze is going to be?

BRO (*in an undertone to Middie*) Next craze?

MIDDIE. When she gets tired of her new sex.

BRO. Oh. As long as she doesn't go back to the motor-scooter.

(*There is a pause*)

MIDDIE. Perhaps we shall be able to have that conversation presently.

BRO. Which conversation?

MIDDIE. Don't you remember we promised ourselves the next time Uncle Ted came up to have a nice long conversation about the conversation we had at the Wordsworths'? When we were all talking about what we'd been talking about at the Hunters' the week before?

BRO. We had the conversation about that last time Uncle Ted was here.

MIDDIE. So we did.

(UNCLE TED *looks up from her book, closes it, and holds it out to Middie*)

BRO. Better?

(MIDDIE *crosses, takes the book and puts it on the tray*)

UNCLE TED. That was just what I wanted, Middie. I felt like some verse after that wretched stuffy compartment.

(MIDDIE *sits on the sofa.* UNCLE TED, *from where she sits, looks across the room through the window into the garden*)

So your elephant came?

MIDDIE. Yes. And look at it.

UNCLE TED (*rising*) Don't you usually have a dwarf elephant? (*She crosses to the window* R *and looks out*)

BRO. They sent us the wrong one.

UNCLE TED. What on earth for?

BRO. We shan't know till we get the measurements from them.

MIDDIE. I can see its great ears flapping about from here.

UNCLE TED. Why didn't you query the measurements when it came?

BRO. We weren't in when they came with it.

MIDDIE. What do they think we want with an elephant that size?

BRO. It's big enough for a hotel.

MIDDIE. People think you're trying to go one better than everybody else.

UNCLE TED (*crossing to the sofa*) Never mind. It's only once a year. (*She sits on the sofa beside Middie*)

BRO. Or a private school. If we had a private school, or a hotel, we might be glad of an elephant that size.

UNCLE TED. You're not calling it "Mr Trench" again, I hope.

BRO. Why not "Mr Trench"?

UNCLE TED. Six years running? You can't call an elephant "Mr Trench" six years running. It looks as if you were hard up for a name to call the animal or something.

BRO. It isn't the same animal every time, you know.

MIDDIE. If it goes berserk in the night, *I'm* not getting up to it.

BRO. As far as that goes it wasn't I who wanted to call it "Mr Trench" the year it was a giraffe.

UNCLE TED. If it's going to go berserk in the night you'd have been better off with a smaller one.

MIDDIE. I'm not getting up to it.

BRO. It was Middie's idea it would make a pleasant change to give the name to a giraffe instead of an elephant.

MIDDIE. I think we'd be better off without it.

UNCLE TED. And be without an elephant at all?

BRO. It seems a bit late now to start complaining about calling it "Mr Trench" six years running.

MIDDIE. I think we'd be better off without an elephant. We've done nothing except bicker ever since they came with it.

(UNCLE TED *takes a cigarette from her handbag, and lights it*)

UNCLE TED. You weren't in when they came with it.

MIDDIE. That's the whole point!

(*There is a silence for a few moments.* BRO *glances through the window*)

BRO. Here's young Bobby coming across the garden.

MIDDIE (*with a glance through the window*) Nora must have sent him. (*She rises and moves towards the door*) She'll have sent him over with the snake.

(MIDDIE *exits, leaving the door open*)

BRO. We're exchanging the elephant with Mrs Mortice. She's letting us have her snake.

UNCLE TED. Won't she need it herself?

BRO. It's too small for her. They sent her the wrong one.

UNCLE TED. I suppose they thought they'd better deal with you both on the same footing.

BRO. They generally do their best to be fair.

UNCLE TED. If they'd sent her the right one after having sent you the wrong one it would have led to all sorts of confusion.

BRO. No. It was Mrs Mortice who got the wrong one delivered first. We were after her.

UNCLE TED. Oh.

BRO. Not that it would have been any less confusing that way, I suppose.

(MIDDIE *enters, carrying a pencil box. She shuts the door, and crosses to Uncle Ted*)

MIDDIE. That was Nora's little boy. He's brought across our boa constrictor, Uncle Ted. (*She hands the box to Uncle Ted*)

(BRO *rises to see better*)

UNCLE TED. Do I open it? (*She slides the lid open*)

BRO (*peering into the box*) That's never a boa constrictor. (*He sits again in the armchair*)

MIDDIE. Don't let it get out of its loose-box. We shall have it eavesdropping.

UNCLE TED (*closing the box and handing it to Middie*) You don't seem to be getting much for your elephant, do you?

MIDDIE (*crossing to the fireplace*) We may decide to have it lengthened. (*She puts the box on the mantelpiece*)

UNCLE TED. Yes. But of course you won't get the thickness then.

(*There is a pause.* MIDDIE *resumes her seat on the sofa*)

BRO. Was it still raining when you went to the door, Middie?

MIDDIE. There's a slight drizzle. It's not much.

BRO. I'll give it a few minutes longer. I don't suppose Nora will mind. I don't go out in the rain oftener than I need these days, Uncle Ted. My old hat isn't up to it.

UNCLE TED. That's what you're always saying, Bro. Isn't he, Middie?

MIDDIE. Hats aren't everything in this world. There are other things besides hats.

BRO. We know they aren't everything.

UNCLE TED. I dare say there are plenty of people who wouldn't mind having a hat like yours, Bro, all the same.

BRO. It isn't so much having the hats as knowing how to make the best use of them.

MIDDIE. We can't all be blessed with hats.

UNCLE TED. I suppose plenty of people do get by without hats, but it's rather silly to pretend they don't matter.

BRO. Look at Mrs Blackboy's husband and the showers he's got through in his time with that green plastic bag he carries round on his head.

MIDDIE. That's not a hat.

BRO. Or Bella for that matter.

MIDDIE. Bella overdoes it. The time she spends on millinery she could spend on something else.

UNCLE TED. She gets through the rain though.

MIDDIE. A lot of those who are supposed to have such wonderful hats go around half the time in other people's.

UNCLE TED. Why don't you weatherproof an old lampshade or something for yourself, Bro?

BRO. I'm not much of a one for millinery, Uncle Ted.

MIDDIE. That sort of thing's all right if you've got millinery in your make-up.

BRO. I've always known what I could do, and I've always known what I couldn't do. That's the reason I never became an air hostess.

MIDDIE. Bro and I prefer to leave the showers to the ones who've got the hats for it.

BRO. The older you get the less hats you seem to have.

Middie. I don't want any more hats than I've got. It's very often the people who bother least about hats who come out of it best whenever there's heavy rain.

Uncle Ted. I've never made any pretensions to hats myself, but I prefer people who've got a few hats to the ones who haven't.

Middie. I can tell you someone who *has* got a good little hat on her head. You've never met Bro's niece, Uncle Ted, have you?

Bro. Oh. Myrtle.

Uncle Ted. Isn't it Myrtle who's just got through her first thunderstorm?

Middie. She sailed right through it just as if she'd got a sou'-wester on.

Bro. I'd like to see her have a try at a hailstorm. She's got the hat for it.

Middie. Don't you put ideas into her head. We don't want her trying to do too much all at once.

Bro. Or a storm at sea.

Middie. She's all right as she is.

Bro. I think that girl's got a sou'-wester hidden away somewhere. You watch. She'll bring it out one of these days and surprise all of us. She looks to me as if she's got her father's sou'-wester.

Middie. Stan never had a sou'-wester in his life. It was his plastic saucer that got him where he was. Anybody would think he was a thorough-going sou'-wester man the way you talk about him.

Bro. It wasn't that he didn't have a sou'-wester so much as that he could never get round to putting it on.

Middie. He never had one. (*To Uncle Ted*) Stan was Bro's brother in the navy, Uncle Ted. (*To Bro*) You know perfectly well he used to borrow quite shamelessly from the other men whenever there was an important storm at sea and he couldn't get by with just his plastic saucer.

Uncle Ted (*loudly*) I'm sure that waste-paper basket of yours has possibilities, Middie.

Middie. Do you like it?

Uncle Ted. It would trim up very nicely for Bro.

MIDDIE. He's had it on. Haven't you, Bro? He tried it on for size. But he won't be seen out in it.

BRO. That sort of thing's all right for the summer.

MIDDIE. Bro hates anything that he thinks makes him look younger.

BRO. I happen to have a death-wish, that's all.

UNCLE TED (*looking at her watch*) We're going to miss the service.

MIDDIE. It's never that time already?

BRO (*rising and crossing to the radio*) We shan't miss much.

MIDDIE. Uncle Ted doesn't want to miss any of it.

(BRO *switches on the radio and tunes it in*)

BRO. It may just have started.

MIDDIE. She's travelled all the way up to Euston for it since four o'clock this morning.

BRO. Sh! (*He crosses and sits in the armchair*)

(*The prayers from the radio gradually become audible.* UNCLE TED *listens with determined seriousness, joining in the responses from time to time.* BRO *and* MIDDIE *listen in a manner suggesting boredom half-heartedly concealed*)

PRAYER. . . . weep at the elastic as it stretches:

RESPONSE. And rejoice that it might have been otherwise.

MIDDIE (*whispering*) We've missed the start.

BRO. Sh!

PRAYER. Let us sing because round things roll:

RESPONSE. And rejoice that it might have been otherwise.

PRAYER. Let us give praise for woodlice and for buildings sixty-nine feet three inches high:

RESPONSE. For Adam Smith's *Wealth of Nations* published in seventeen seventy-six.

PRAYER. For the fifth key from the left on the lower manual of the organ of the Church of the Ascension in the Piazza Vittorio Emanuele the Second in the town of Castelfidardo in Italy:

RESPONSE. And for bats.

PRAYER. Let us give praise for those who compile

dictionaries in large, rambling buildings, for the suitably clad men and women on our commons and in our hotels, for all those who in the fullness of time will go out to meet whatever fate awaits them; for the tall, the ham-fisted, the pompous; and for all men everywhere and at all times:

RESPONSE. Amen.

PRAYER. And now let us dwell upon drugs, for their effects enlighten us; upon judo and hypnosis, for their effects enlighten us; upon privation and upon loneliness, upon the heat of the sun and the silence of deserts; upon torture, upon interrogation, upon death—for their effects enlighten us:

RESPONSE. Give us light, that we may be enlightened.

PRAYER. Give us light upon the nature of our know-ing; for the illusions of the sane man are not the illusions of the lunatic, and the illusions of the flagellant are not the illusions of the alcholic, and the illusions of the delirious are not the illusions of the lovesick, and the illusions of the genius are not the illusions of the common man:

RESPONSE. Give us light, that we may be enlightened.

PRAYER. Give us light, that, sane, we may attain to a distortion more acceptable than the lunatic's and call it truth:

RESPONSE. That, sane, we may call it truth and know it to be false.

PRAYER. That, sane, we may know ourselves, and by knowing ourselves may know what it is we know:

RESPONSE. Amen.

(*There is a pause*)

MIDDIE. That was rather nice.

(*The introductory bars of "Sweet Polly Oliver" in a metrical version are heard through the radio*)

UNCLE TED (*rising*) This is where we stand.

(*Bro and* MIDDIE *rise.* UNCLE TED *joins softly in the hymn-like singing. As* MIDDIE *becomes aware of this, she surreptitiously draws* BRO's *attention to it, and both suppress their amusement. When the singing ends, there is a momentary silence, and then all begin to be excessively normal by way of neutralizing their embarrassment.* UNCLE TED *and* MIDDIE *resume their seats on the sofa.* BRO *crosses to the radio*)

VOICE (*from the radio*) This evening's service, from the Church of the Hypothetical Imperative in Brinkfall, was conducted by Father Gerontius.

(BRO *switches off the radio*)

MIDDIE. It's a pity we missed the first part.

BRO (*sitting in the armchair*) At any rate we got the last part.

MIDDIE. Naturally we got it.

BRO. Why naturally?

MIDDIE. It isn't so very easy once you've switched it on to miss the last part, is it?

BRO. Not if we switched it off too soon?

UNCLE TED. We didn't miss much of it. How did you both enjoy it? I thought it was very good.

MIDDIE. It was a lot better this week. Didn't you think so, Bro? It hasn't been at all uplifting the last few weeks.

BRO. They can't expect to keep it up week after week. They ought to give it a rest for a time.

MIDDIE. Of course, I think you got more of a real, good worship, if you know what I mean, in the old days when they weren't afraid to let themselves go with idols and things.

UNCLE TED. You're both getting jaded. If you were to come to it fresh after a few weeks without any service at all, you'd be surprised what a difference it would make. You'd be as inspired as anything by it. It's made *me* feel thoroughly uplifted, anyway.

BRO. Isn't it rather a long journey for you, though— every time you want to hear the service? Travelling up to Euston from four o'clock in the morning?

UNCLE TED. What's the alternative? It would mean having a radio down there.

BRO. I suppose it would.

UNCLE TED. Besides, I like to come up occasionally. The only trouble about that is that it's such a long journey; and if I come here it hardly leaves me time to get back. (*She looks at her watch*)

BRO. When's your train, Uncle Ted?

UNCLE TED. It leaves Euston at nine. I shall have to be off soon.

MIDDIE. Not until you've had another read. I'm not letting you go out on a miserable two stanzas. It won't take me long to get down some more books. (*She rises and goes to the bookshelves*)

UNCLE TED. Thank you, Middie—but I really oughtn't to stop for another read.

BRO (*rising*) You're going to stay and get some prose inside you first. Don't get those down, Middie. I've got some others outside.

MIDDIE (*moving to the sofa*) He's got a special little store out there, for when anybody comes unexpectedly. I expect he'll bring in one of the new books on the physical nature of the universe. (*She sits on the sofa*)

(BRO *enters with three new books, and a pair of scissors*)

BRO. You've got time for a dip in one of these before you go. (*He puts the books on the sideboard and, opening one of them, begins cutting out part of a page with the scissors*)

UNCLE TED. Just a paragraph, then, Bro.

MIDDIE. You won't get anything like this in the Queen's Road. Will she, Bro.

UNCLE TED. That's surely not for me, Bro? I shall never finish it in time.

BRO (*indicating with the scissors a shorter passage*) How about that, then? You can't have anything shorter than that—it's only a paragraph.

UNCLE TED. That's fine, thanks, Bro. He was going to give me nearly half a page, Middie.

BRO. You may want some of this with it. (*He fetches a large dictionary from the bookshelf and puts it on the coffee-table*) But try it neat first of all.

MIDDIE. What's that you're offering her with it, Bro?

BRO. It's just a dictionary. She can take the edge off it, if she finds it too strong, with a definition or two.

UNCLE TED. I'll try it without first.

(BRO *hands a cutting to Uncle Ted*)

Thank you, Bro.

BRO. Do you want one, Middie?

MIDDIE. Of course I want one.

(BRO *takes two cuttings, hands one to Middie, keeps the other for himself, then sits in the armchair*)

Well, let's hope it won't be so long next time before we see you, Uncle Ted.

(*All raise their cuttings*)

UNCLE TED. Cheers.

BRO
MIDDIE } (*together*) Cheers.

(*All read, looking up abstractedly from time to time*)

UNCLE TED (*lowering her cutting*) Well—it's certainly got a kick to it. (*She puts the cutting on the coffee-table*)

BRO (*raising his eyes momentarily*) I was hoping you'd like it.

MIDDIE (*putting her cutting on the coffee-table*) You didn't find it too strong, then?

UNCLE TED. I thought it was just right, Middie.

BRO (*putting his cutting on the floor*) Why should she find it too strong? It's supposed to have a bit of a bite to it.

UNCLE TED. Is it my imagination—or could I detect monosyllables in it?

BRO. Ah—I wondered if you'd spot the monosyllables. They do give it just that extra something, I think. Middie thinks they spoil it, but . . .

UNCLE TED. Oh, no—it needed just that flavouring of monosyllables to give it a tang. But you shouldn't have cut into a new book, Bro. (*She rises, picks up her gloves and handbag and prepares to leave*)

MIDDIE (*rising*) It isn't often we have the opportunity, Uncle Ted. You mustn't leave it so long next time.

BRO (*rising*) You know you're very welcome to come up here for the service any time you feel you need uplifting.

UNCLE TED. I must try and get up a bit oftener. It's that awful long journey; if only there were some way of getting round that.

MIDDIE. Couldn't you make a detour?

UNCLE TED. I'd never get here, Middie. Thanks for the read, Bro—and the service. I shall have to be off.

MIDDIE. She'll miss her train.

BRO. Yes—well, good-bye, then, Uncle Ted. Have a good journey.

UNCLE TED. Good-bye, Bro.

MIDDIE. Have you got everything?

UNCLE TED. Yes, I left my cases out in the hall.

(UNCLE TED *exits, followed by* MIDDIE, *who closes the door behind her, leaving Bro alone.* BRO *gets a tray of stamps, etc. from the sideboard and sits in the armchair.* MIDDIE *re-enters*)

BRO. We forgot to ask about the motor-scooter.

MIDDIE. She's sold it. (*She sits on the sofa*)

BRO. When did she say that?

MIDDIE. I asked her about it in the hall. She said she'd sold it to a salesman.

(*There is a pause*)

BRO. The last time she was here she told us she'd bought it.

(*There is a pause*)

MIDDIE. Oh—Bro. On the news this morning—I meant to tell you—they gave the figure as eight million.

BRO. No!

MIDDIE. That was the figure they gave. He said that a normal female cod could be the mother of eight million eggs.

BRO. Not eight million!

MIDDIE. I thought myself it seemed rather a lot.

BRO. It's irresponsibility run riot.

C

(*There is a pause*)

Who on earth do they hope to get to count eight million eggs?

MIDDIE. And they're such fiddling things to count.

BRO. Not only that—it would take eight hundred thousand pairs of hands before you'd have enough fingers to count them on. You couldn't do it with less.

MIDDIE. I don't know I'm sure.

BRO. Eight hundred thousand people to count the eggs of a single cod. It's ludicrous.

MIDDIE. That was the figure they gave on the news.

(*There is a pause*)

It's Aunt Chloe's birthday next week.

BRO (*abstractedly*) We shall have to try and think of something for her.

(*There is a pause*)

MIDDIE. There's a brand-new deaf-aid upstairs. We've never used it.

BRO. Aunt Chloe hasn't been deaf for years.

(*There is a pause*)

It's the same whatever you think of, for that matter. Either she's got it or she doesn't need it. And she certainly doesn't need a deaf-aid.

(*There is a pause*)

MIDDIE. Unless we were to burst a paper bag in her ear?

(*There is a pause*)

BRO. You wouldn't do any good with a paper bag.

(*There is a pause*)

We should have to get a blank cartridge and fire that.

MIDDIE. I don't think she'd really expect anything as elaborate as that.

BRO. I wasn't suggesting we should do it.

MIDDIE. It would look a bit ostentatious.

BRO. I was only saying that that would be how we should have to do it if we were going to do it at all.

MIDDIE. After all, it isn't as if it's her twenty-first.

(*There is a pause*)

You won't forget you've got an elephant to deliver, Bro?

BRO. No. I was just reading in the paper here— apparently what they said at the elementary school is true about four going into twenty five times.

MIDDIE. I should want to see it first.

BRO. It's no good just dismissing it as textbook talk, Middie. It wouldn't be in the paper unless there was something in it.

MIDDIE. No, I suppose not.

(*There is a pause*)

BRO. I suppose I'd better get round to Nora's with the elephant. (*He rises, puts the tray on the sideboard and goes to the door*) Where are my gumboots?

MIDDIE. What do you want gumboots for to go down the road a few doors with an elephant? Where are your other shoes?

BRO. I'm not going without my gumboots.

MIDDIE. For goodness' sake get them on, then, and go.

(BRO *goes into the hall, picks up a pair of gumboots and comes into the room*)

BRO. If you switch on the radio while I'm out you can listen to the play. (*He sits on the upstage arm of the armchair, takes off his shoes and puts on the gumboots*)

MIDDIE. How long are you going to be?

BRO. You'll get the last half-hour or so of it. I don't know how long I shall be—it depends whether I meet Mrs Stencil on the way.

MIDDIE. For goodness' sake go the other way then. We don't want Mrs Stencil asking a lot of questions.

BRO. She won't be out at this time.

MIDDIE. This is just when she will be out. She always

goes out in the evening exercising her butterflies.

BRO. I thought they were in quarantine? (*He rises*)

MIDDIE. They came out of quarantine weeks ago. She's had the vet to them since then.

BRO (*moving to the door*) Well—if I meet her, I meet her.

MIDDIE. Try not to let her see the elephant.

BRO. I certainly shan't draw attention to it. (*He stands in the open doorway*) You'd better get up to bed if I'm late.

MIDDIE. *Up* to bed? I thought we were living in a bungalow?

(BRO *looks bewilderedly around, then exits to the hall closing the door behind him.* MIDDIE *leans over to the radio, switches it on then works on her rug-making.* BRO's *and* MIDDIE's *voices are heard through the radio*)

BRO's VOICE. It was your idea it would make a pleasant change to give the name to a sea-lion instead of a dinosaur.

MIDDIE's VOICE. We've done nothing except bicker since they came with it.

(*The telephone rings*)

BRO's VOICE. We weren't in when they came with it.

(MIDDIE *rises*)

MIDDIE's VOICE. That's the whole point.

(MIDDIE *switches off the radio, crosses to the telephone and lifts the receiver*)

MIDDIE (*into the telephone*) Mrs Paradock . . . Oh, Mrs Stencil . . . Yes . . . No, Bro's just this moment gone out . . . Yes . . . Yes . . . Yes, I can imagine . . . Of course it is . . . Of course . . . Yes . . . Yes . . . Oh, but I think they get used to it, Mrs Stencil, don't they? . . . They get a sort of head for heights . . . I really don't think heights worry them, Mrs Stencil . . . Some birds, perhaps—but not eagles . . . Oh, yes. Eagles do . . . Yes . . . But it must be very rare, however high they fly . . . It must be very rare for an eagle to come

over dizzy . . . Yes . . . Yes . . . But wouldn't that give
them the feeling of being rather hampered? . . . Yes . . .
But I do think an eagle likes to swoop down some-
times . . . But not if it's wearing a parachute . . . Oh, I
can understand how you feel, Mrs Stencil . . . Yes . . .
Yes . . . (*Hesitantly*) I'm afraid it would have to be more
or less a token subscription this time—this is always our
expensive quarter . . . No, naturally . . . No . . . Anyway, I'll tell Bro when he comes in, and . . . Yes . . .
Yes . . . I suppose they must . . . It's the peering down,
I expect . . . Yes . . . They must be peering down
most of the time . . . And of course with some of
them they're supposed to stare into the sun as well,
aren't they? . . . Don't eagles stare at the sun? . . .
Yes . . . Still, I should think if they found that . . . Yes . . .
But if they found it was becoming a strain on their eyes
they'd surely stop doing it . . . Yes . . . But I doubt
whether they'd take the trouble to wear them once the
novelty had worn off . . . Oh, they are—they're very
expensive. Even the steel-rimmed ones . . . Yes . . .
Yes . . . A kind of Welfare State for animals, in fact . . .
Yes—well, I'll tell Bro, Mrs Stencil, when he comes in
and . . . Yes . . . Yes, I will, Mrs Stencil . . . Good-bye.
(*She replaces the receiver, switches on the radio, then sits on the
sofa*)

(BRO's *and* MIDDIE's VOICES *are heard through the
radio*)

MIDDIE's VOICE. What do you want gumboots for to
go down the road a few doors with a dinosaur? Where
are your other shoes?

BRO's VOICE. I'm not going without my gumboots.

MIDDIE's VOICE. For goodness' sake get them on,
then, and go.

(BRO *enters, wearing his gumboots. The voices on the
radio give way to interval music.* BRO *closes the door, sits
in the armchair and takes off his gumboots*)

MIDDIE. You didn't stay at Nora's long. (*She switches
off the radio*)

BRO. I didn't stay at Nora's at all. Where are my slippers?

MIDDIE. Mrs Stencil rang up.

BRO (*putting on his shoes*) Oh? What is it this time? Emergency breathing apparatus for deep-sea fish again?

MIDDIE. Apparently she's still on the Appeals Committee for the Birds of Prey Protection League.

BRO. I'm not putting my hand in my pocket every few weeks for that. And you can tell her I said so. Birds of prey! They're just as capable of looking after themselves as we are.

MIDDIE. That's what I said to Mrs Stencil. Besides, what do eagles want with parachutes?

BRO. Is that what she's collecting for?

MIDDIE. Or any other bird for that matter. She's got it into her head they need to have some kind of safety equipment.

BRO. They've got their two wings, haven't they?

MIDDIE. Mrs Stencil's worried what would happen if they were to get cramp or anything while they were up there.

BRO. She fusses.

MIDDIE. I think she's hoping that if the League can provide a few parachutes out of their own funds, she might be able . . .

BRO. Out of *our* funds.

MIDDIE. She's hoping she might get the authorities interested in supplying spectacles for them.

BRO. For whom?

MIDDIE. For the eagles and things. I told her I didn't think many of them would bother wearing glasses once the novelty had worn off.

(*There is a pause.* BRO *picks up his newspaper and reads*)

It's the height they have to peer down from before they swoop. She thinks it puts too much strain on their eyes.

BRO. They don't have to peer down. They're free agents.

MIDDIE. That's what I said to her.

Bro. Parachutes. Glasses. They get too much done for them.

(*There is a pause*)

Was that the play you were listening to when I came in?

Middie. You didn't want it, did you? I switched it off.

Bro. We may as well see how it ends.

(Middie *switches on the radio and takes up her rug.* Bro *continues to be occupied with the newspaper.* Middie's *and* Bro's *voices are heard through the radio*)

Middie's Voice. And what did Edna say?

Bro's Voice. I didn't get as far as Edna's.

Middie's Voice. Where have you been, then?

Bro's Voice. I've been in the garden.

Middie's Voice. Not all the time? (*She pauses*) In the garden doing what?

Bro's Voice (*exasperated*) In the garden trying to get that blasted dinosaur through the gate!

Middie's Voice. Really! (*She pauses*) I'm going out to make a drink for myself. (*She pauses*) What are *you* having—coffee? Or cocoa?

Bro's Voice. Hot milk.

(*The interval music is heard again.* Middie *switches off the radio*)

Bro (*gloomily*) What was the rest of it like?

Middie. You didn't miss much.

(Middie *takes up her rug.* Bro *reads. A long silence intervenes*)

And what did Nora say?

Bro. I didn't get as far as Nora's.

Middie. You've been out there for hours. What have you been doing?

Bro. I've been in the garden.

Middie. Not all the time?

Bro. I was out there for less than twenty minutes and

I shouldn't have met with any more success if I'd been out there all night.

MIDDIE. I don't know what you're talking about.

BRO. I'm talking about that bloody elephant!

MIDDIE. Bro!

BRO. How do you expect me or anybody else to get a whacking great oaf of an elephant through a gate wide enough to take a pram?

(MIDDIE *puts down her rug and is about to go, tight-lipped, to the door*)

MIDDIE (*rising; conclusively*) It was got *in*. (*She moves to the door*) What are you having to drink? Cocoa? Or coffee?

(MIDDIE *pauses at the door, and turns in the act of going out as she waits in tightly-reined impatience for Bro's answer. BRO is still under the influence of his own irritation, so that some seconds pass before he registers Middie's question. When he does so, he reflects for a moment before answering*)

BRO. Hot milk.

CURTAIN

FURNITURE AND PROPERTY LIST

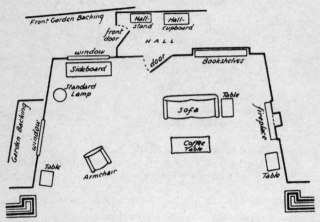

On stage : Sideboard. *On it :* bottles, 2 small adjustable spanners, tray with stamps, etc.

Armchair (RC) *On it :* cushion, newspaper

Sofa. *On it :* cushions

Small table (L of sofa) *On it :* radio

Under it : 2 bottles

Low coffee-table. *On it :* basket with books, *Woman
and Home* magazine, ashtray, rug-making
materials

Small table (down L) *On it :* telephone

Small table (down R)

Fire-irons

Fire-grate

Scuttle with coal

Bookshelves. *In them :* books, dictionary

On floor by bookshelves : tray

On mantelpiece : pipe

Over mantelpiece : mirror

Standard lamp

2 pairs window curtains
Carpet on floor
Pictures on walls
In hall: hall cupboard
         hat-stand. *On it:* hats and coats, torn and
         dirty raincoat
         pair of gumboots
Other suitable dressing as desired

Off stage: Telegram (MIDDIE)
         Case (UNCLE TED)
         Pencil-box (MIDDIE)
         3 new books (BRO)
         Pair of scissors (BRO)

Personal: BRO: pouch with tobacco, matches
         UNCLE TED: watch, gloves, handbag. *In it:* packet
         of cigarettes, lighter

LIGHTING PLOT

Property fittings required: standard lamp, fire
    Interior. A living-room. The same scene throughout
    THE MAIN ACTING AREAS are at an armchair RC, and at a
        sofa LC
    THE APPARENT SOURCES OF LIGHT are windows R and L
        of the back wall

To open: Effect of early evening, dull daylight
          Fire on
          Lamp off
          Flood outside door up C, on

No cues

EFFECTS PLOT

*Printed in Great Britain
by Butler & Tanner Ltd, Frome and London*